# GRUMPY DINOSAUR

by Michael Gordon

THIS BOOK BELONGS TO

..............................................................................

..............................................................................

Leo's best friend is a
dinosaur named Sonny;

He's usually kind and he
thinks that he's funny.

There's only one problem
that Leo can see:

Sonny sometimes gets
grumpy, unfortunately.

The dinosaur gets mad when
things don't go his way;

He explodes like "dino-mite"
several times a day.

Leo is still teaching him
to play nice and share;

Their friendship is special;
he tells Sonny he cares.

Today, at the park, Sonny's mood got quite nasty;

He was kicking up dirt and swinging from trees.

He ran up the slide while the children slid down;

He made Jazlyn cry when he acted like a clown.

Some folks didn't like it,
didn't think it was funny;

They told him to stop and
tried to reason with Sonny.

The parents didn't think Sonny
should get his own way,

So, he stomped off in a
tantrum and refused to play.

He waved his arms and
shouted; he got very loud;

The ruckus attracted
a sizeable crowd.

They told him to go as they
pointed and stared.

"Come back when you're
polite and willing to share."

Later, at dinner, when
they sat down to eat,

Sonny didn't want salad,
he didn't want meat.

"I hate vegetables," he said.
"I want dessert first!"

He was still acting badly,
he was acting his worst.

Leo tried to calm Sonny,
but he just walked away,

Then dumped toys out in the
bedroom and started to play.

He was alone for a while
before Leo walked in.

"I want to talk to you," he said,
"and you need to listen."

M
O
N
A
D
R

"No one wants to be around
a dinosaur that's mean.

You only think of yourself so
the children aren't keen

To play with you. And another
thing that's not good:

You hurt my mom's feelings
when you insult her food."

Sonny considered the problem;
he thought long and hard.

He didn't want to play by
himself in the backyard.

He had fun at the park where
the neighbor kids play.

He vowed to be nicer; he
would change his bad ways.

He said sorry to Mom and Dad, and to Leo too.

"I shouldn't have shouted, I don't want to hurt you.

I'll stop being grumpy, I'll quit being my worst.

From now on I'll play nicely and eat my vegetables first."

# About author

Michael Gordon is the talented author of several highly rated children's books including the popular Sleep Tight, Little Monster, and the Animal Bedtime.

He collaborates with the renowned Kids Book Book that creates picture books for all of ages to enjoy. Michael's goal is to create books that are engaging, funny, and inspirational for children of all ages and their parents.

# Contact

For all other questions about books or author, please e-mail michaelgordonclub@gmail.com.

# Award-winning books

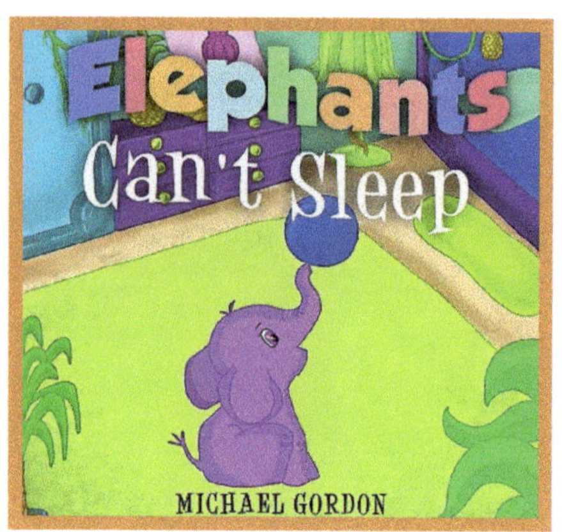


## Elephants Can not Sleep

The

Little Elephant likes to break the rules. He never cleans his room. He never listens to mama's bedtime stories and goes to bed really late. But what if he tried to follow the routine so that the bedtime would become an amazing experience?

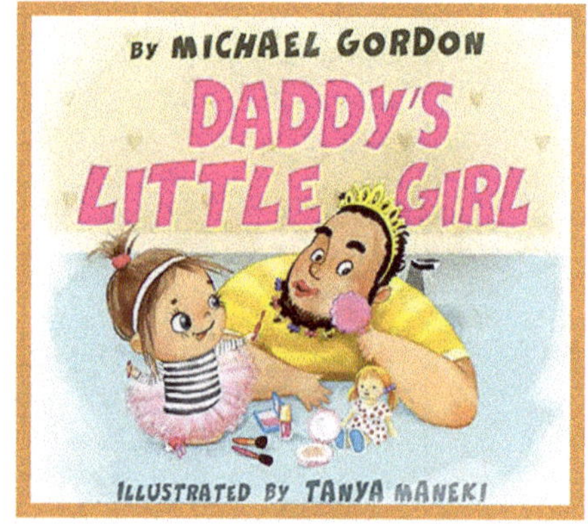


## Little Girl's Daddy

the Who Needs a super hero the when you have your dad? Written in beautiful rhyme this is an excellent story that honors all fathers in the world.

## The Goodnight Kiss

Welcome to a cozy, sweet little bunny family. Mom is putting her little son Ben to bed, but she's not quite successful. Little boy still wants to play games and stay up late. Ben also likes to keep his mommy in his room at bedtime. Mrs. Bunny tries milk, warm blankets, books , and finally a kiss ... what will work?

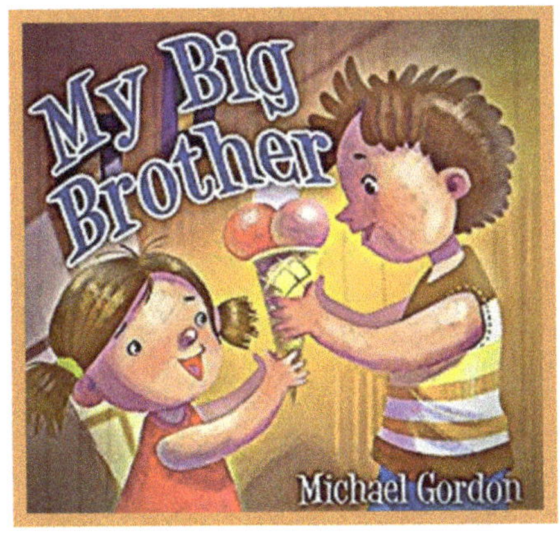


## My Big Brother

The

Each of our lives will always be a special part of the other. There's Nothing Quite Like A Sibling Bond Written in beautiful rhyme this is an excellent story that values patience, acceptance and bond between a brother and his sister.

Thank You!

For purchasing this book,

I'd like to give you a free gift

An amazing bedtime story for your child

https://michaelgordonclub.wixsite.com/books

CPSIA information can be obtained
at www.ICGtesting.com
Printed in the USA
LVHW070847141121
703286LV00008B/656